SCIENCE SKILLS 3

T0007130

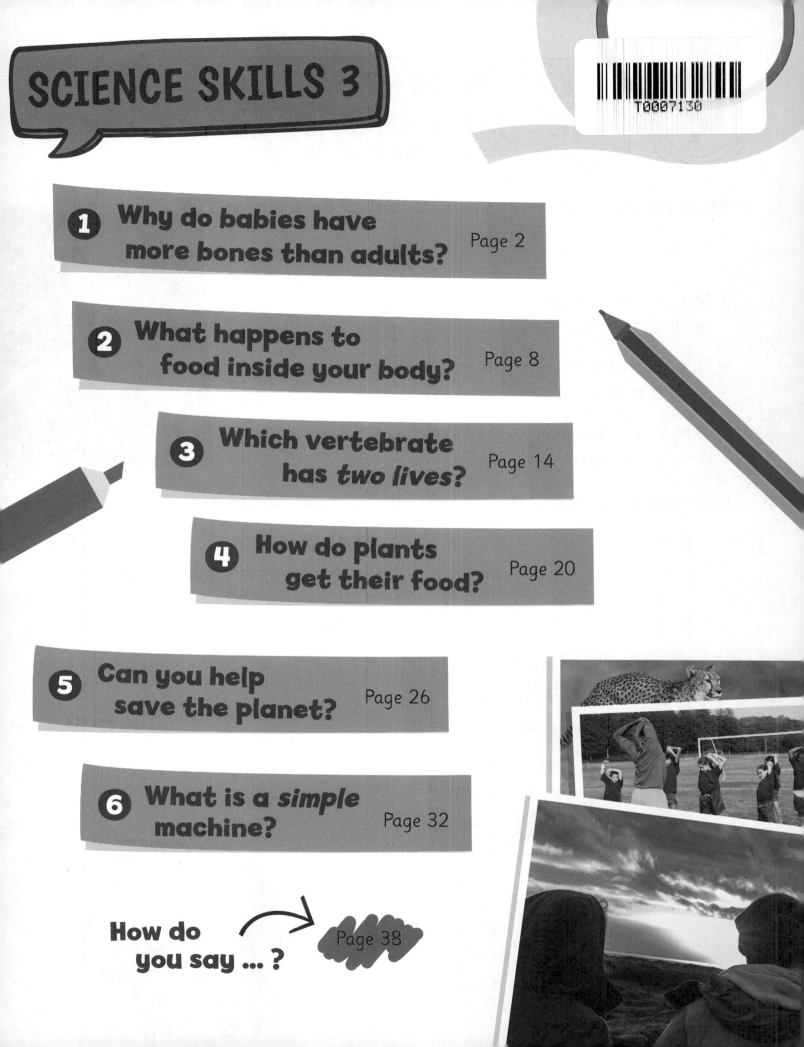

WHY DO BABIES HAVE MORE BONES THAN ADULTS?

1 Write the words from the box next to their descriptions.

brain   sense organs   nervous system

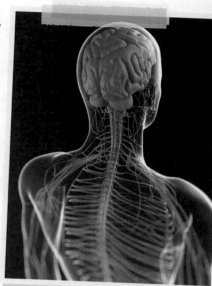

a This body system controls our voluntary and involuntary actions. _____

b This organ is the control centre of our nervous system. _____

c They send information to the brain through the nerves. _____

2 Complete the crossword about the nervous system.

ACROSS

1 This part of the brain controls involuntary actions.

DOWN

2 This part of the brain controls voluntary actions.

3 These carry information to and from the brain.

4 This part of the brain controls balance and coordination.

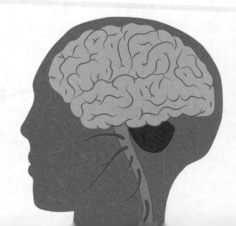

3 Complete the sentences using the words in the box.

bones   soft   rigid   ~~locomotor~~   hard   elastic   joints

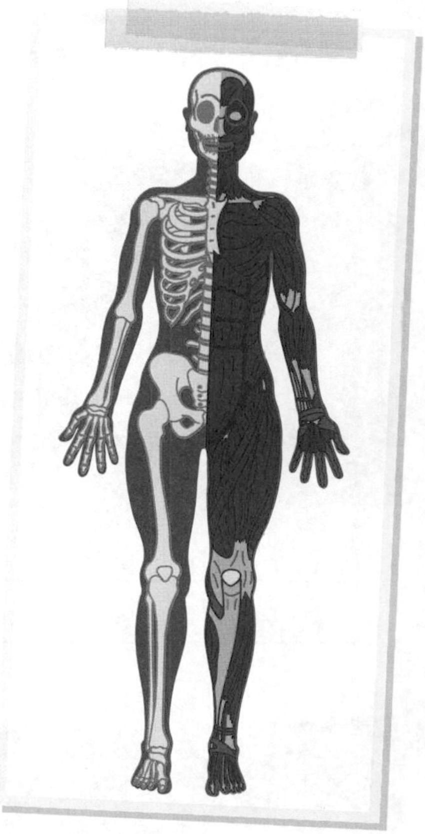

a Our _locomotor_ system allows us to move.

b Our bones are _____ and _____ .

c Our muscles are _____ and _____ .

d Our skeleton is made up of _____ .

e Our bones are connected at the _____ .

4 Circle the joints.

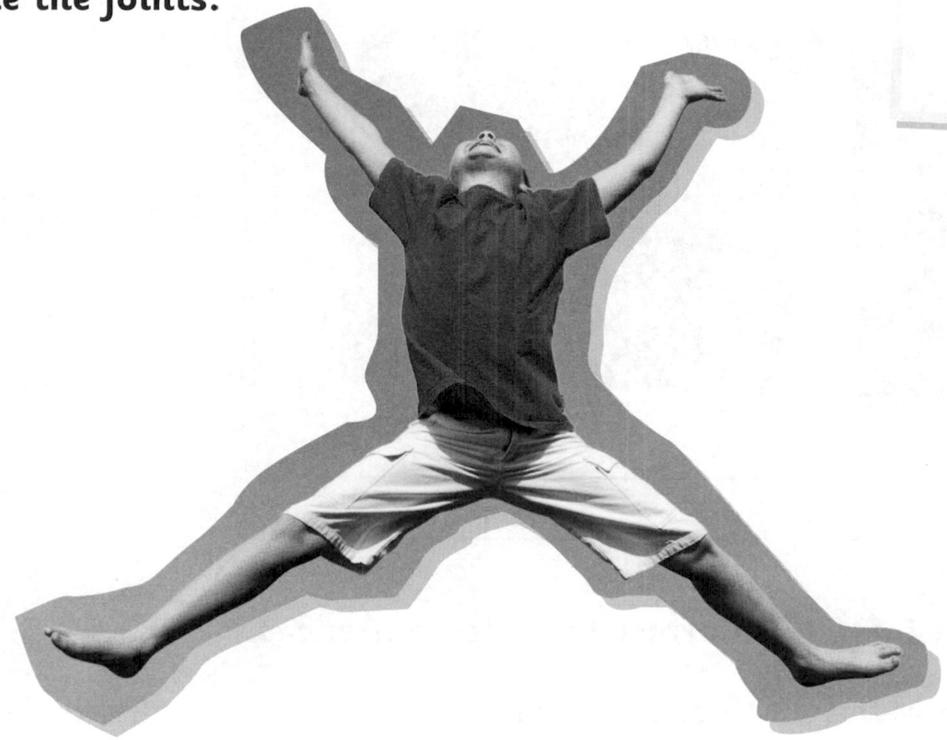

5 What do our senses perceive? Complete the chart using the words in the box.

soft   quiet   blue   ~~disgusting~~   rough   loud   big   delicious

Sight	Hearing	Smell and taste	Touch
		disgusting	

3

6 Write sentences about the pictures. Use the example to help you.

a My nose is the organ
of smell.

7 Circle true (T) or false (F). Correct the false sentences.

a Sound waves enter the ear through the middle ear.   T / **F**

Sound waves enter the ear through the outer ear.

b Sound waves make the eardrum vibrate.   T / F

_____

c Loud sounds cannot damage the ear.   T / F

_____

d Earwax protects the ear from infections.   T / F

_____

8 Find the parts of the eye in the wordsearch.

F	N	V	C	X	R	Z	S	A	R	G
C	O	R	P	F	E	Y	E	L	I	D
R	L	C	U	J	T	H	Y	H	G	F
S	F	V	P	F	I	G	E	A	P	E
U	I	R	I	S	N	W	B	S	O	R
A	N	B	L	D	A	H	R	D	I	T
U	T	N	X	C	R	J	O	F	U	W
T	I	M	Z	T	Y	L	W	G	Y	Q
W	A	E	Y	E	L	A	S	H	E	S

9 Label the photo with the words from Activity 8.

a _____

b _____

c _____

d _____

e _____

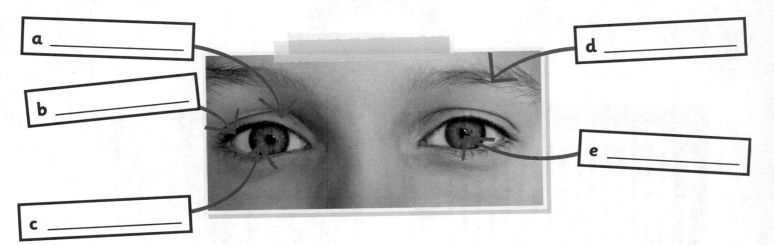

10 Complete the lines and draw the image on the retina.

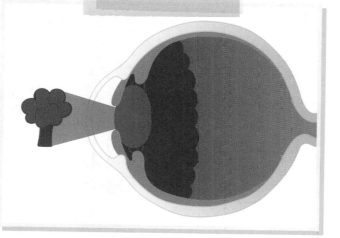

The image on
the retina is

_____ .

11 Complete the table with different foods.

Sweet	Salty	Bitter	Sour
strawberry		celery	

12 Look and read. Choose the correct words and write them on the lines.

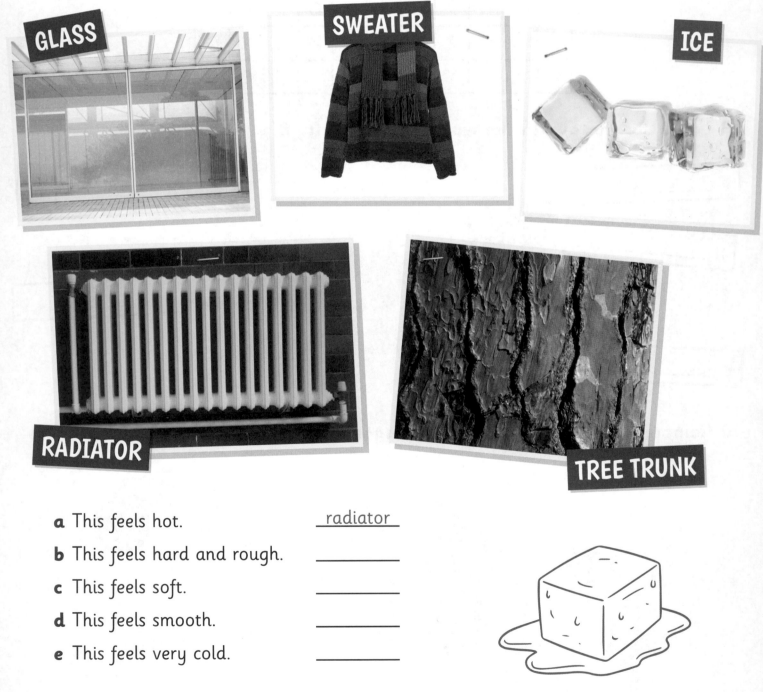

GLASS

SWEATER

ICE

RADIATOR

TREE TRUNK

a This feels hot. <u>radiator</u>

b This feels hard and rough. _____

c This feels soft. _____

d This feels smooth. _____

e This feels very cold. _____

13 Read the text. Choose the right words and write them on the lines.

Look after your locomotor system.

a Warm up before you do ___exercise___ .

b Try not to carry a heavy _____ .

c _____ properly on your chair.

d Do not play _____ for too long.

e Be careful when you are _____ in the playground.

a homework · exercise · English

b school bag · pencil · sandwich

c Swing · Stand · Sit

d video games · homework · exercise

e talking · running · laughing

14 Match to make complete sentences.

a The iris is the

b Sensory nerves send

c Taste buds are found

d An upside-down image

e The skin is the

○ organ of touch.

○ is formed on the retina.

○ coloured part of the eye.

○ information about how things feel to the brain.

○ on the tongue and detect different tastes.

WHAT HAPPENS TO FOOD INSIDE YOUR BODY?

1 Which groups do these foods belong to? Complete the chart using the words in the box.

~~avocado~~   cheese   fish   rice   lettuce   olive oil
pasta   chicken   yoghurt   apple

Fruits and vegetables	Dairy	Carbohydrates and fibre	Proteins and iron	Fats
				avocado

2 Unscramble the letters to find the names of the nutrients.

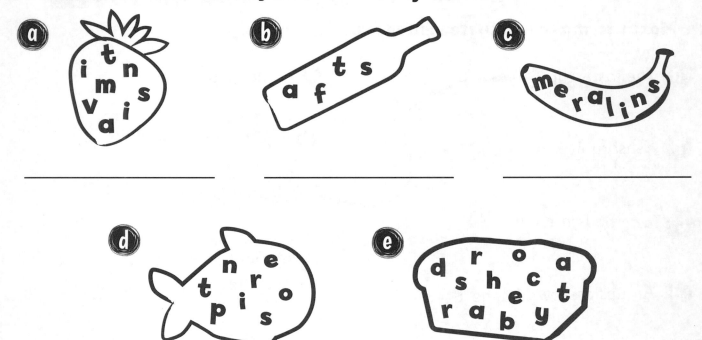

3 Label the foods with the nutrients they give us.

carbohydrates   proteins   vitamins   calcium   fats

a _____

b _____

c _____

d _____

e _____

4 Find the nutrients in the wordsearch. Then, write the words below their descriptions.

A	V	C	Z	A	C	A	L	C	I	U	M	H
F	I	V	M	P	E	Y	P	O	H	L	T	D
D	T	B	N	R	S	U	G	F	J	G	H	A
C	A	R	B	O	H	Y	D	R	A	T	E	S
G	M	N	V	T	F	H	W	B	D	T	U	X
H	I	M	P	E	H	G	E	V	F	A	S	B
J	N	E	Y	I	J	A	F	I	B	R	E	R
K	S	R	T	N	R	N	Y	H	Z	A	V	W
R	W	Y	E	S	E	B	T	U	E	Y	F	S
T	Q	U	I	O	P	Q	W	E	R	T	D	A

a This nutrient is good for our nervous system.

_____

b This nutrient keeps our bones and teeth healthy.

_____

c This nutrient gives us energy.

_____

d This nutrient is good for our digestive system.

_____

e This nutrient makes our muscles strong and helps us grow.

_____

5 **Write the names of the body systems in the pictures.**
Then, write the names next to the definitions.

| circulatory system | respiratory system | excretory system |

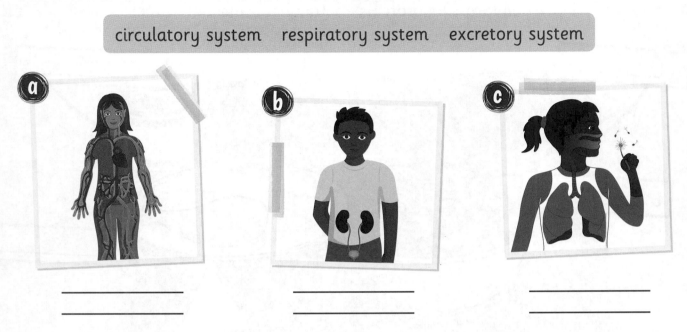

a _____

b _____

c _____

1 This body system takes in air through the mouth and nose. _____

2 This body system transports oxygen and nutrients to all
parts of the body.   _____

3 This body system eliminates liquid waste from the body.   _____

6 **Order the stages of digestion.**

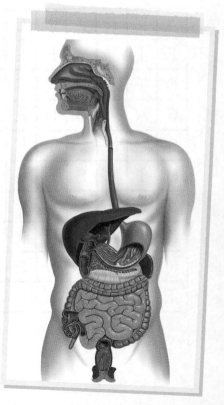

| 1 | In the mouth, the teeth break the food down into smaller pieces. |

☐ The waste moves to the large intestine.

☐ The oesophagus pushes the food down
into the stomach.

☐ The nutrients pass from the small intestine
into the blood.

☐ The small intestine separates the nutrients
from the waste.

☐ The blood transports the nutrients to all
parts of the body.

7 Label the heart.

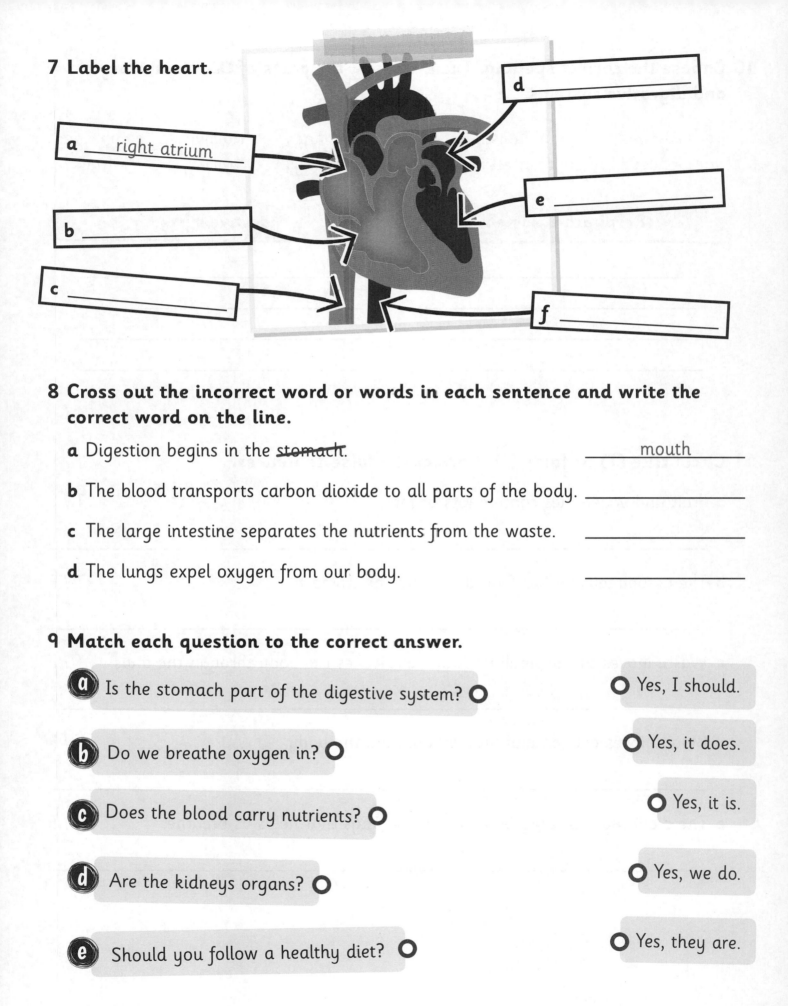

a ___right atrium___

b _____

c _____

d _____

e _____

f _____

8 Cross out the incorrect word or words in each sentence and write the correct word on the line.

a Digestion begins in the ~~stomach~~.   _____mouth_____

b The blood transports carbon dioxide to all parts of the body. _____

c The large intestine separates the nutrients from the waste.   _____

d The lungs expel oxygen from our body.   _____

9 Match each question to the correct answer.

a Is the stomach part of the digestive system? ○   ○ Yes, I should.

b Do we breathe oxygen in? ○   ○ Yes, it does.

c Does the blood carry nutrients? ○   ○ Yes, it is.

d Are the kidneys organs? ○   ○ Yes, we do.

e Should you follow a healthy diet? ○   ○ Yes, they are.

10 Choose the correct spelling. Then, classify the parts of the respiratory and digestive systems.

| oesophagus | small intestine | annus | langs | trachea | diaphragm |
| oesophegus | small intestinne | anus | lungs | trakea | diafragm |

Respiratory system	Digestive system
_____	_____
_____	_____
_____	_____
_____	_____

11 Circle true (T) or false (F). Correct the false sentences.

a Fruit and vegetables contain lots of fats.   T / F

_____

b The oesophagus pushes food down into the stomach.   T / F

_____

c Waste moves to the small intestine and leaves the body through the anus.   T / F

_____

d Blood moves oxygen and nutrients around the body.   T / F

_____

e The diaphragm is a big bone under the lungs that helps us breathe.   T / F

_____

12 Circle the odd one out. Explain why it is different.

a stomach – intestines – heart – mouth _____

_____

b diaphragm – trachea – lungs – ventricles _____

_____

c lungs – bladder – urethra – kidney _____

_____

13 Look at the picture and read the text. Then, write words to complete the sentences about the text.

Look after your teeth.

Young children have 20 teeth. These teeth are called 'milk teeth'. When we are six years old, our milk teeth begin to fall out. Then, our permanent teeth begin to grow. Adults have 32 teeth. They are bigger than milk teeth.

We must look after our teeth. Brush them with toothpaste after eating and do not eat too many sweet things. Sugar is very bad for your teeth and can cause cavities.

Visit your dentist regularly. The dentist will make sure that your teeth are healthy and growing correctly.

Do not forget that calcium is good for your teeth and bones, so remember to drink milk and eat dairy products every day.

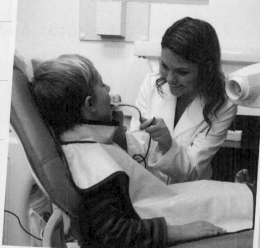

Questions

a When we are six our milk teeth begin _____to fall out_____ .

b Adults have _____ teeth.

c Brush your teeth _____ after eating.

d Do not eat _____ things.

e Visit _____ regularly.

f Drink milk and _____ every day.

13

WHICH VERTEBRATE HAS *TWO LIVES?*

1 Classify the vertebrates. Complete the chart using the words in the box.

~~toad~~ shark horse frog penguin turtle
gorilla duck chameleon carp

Mammals	Birds	Reptiles	Amphibians	Fish
			toad	

2 Look at the photos and write *viviparous* or *oviparous*.

3 Match the definitions to the terms.

a These animals eat other animals. ○   ○ oviparous

b These animals eat plants. ○   ○ omnivores

c These animals eat both plants and other animals. ○   ○ carnivores

d These animals lay eggs. ○   ○ viviparous

e These animals' babies are born live. ○   ○ herbivores

4 Write sentences about the characteristics of mammals. Use the photos to help you.

a Classification:
<u>Mammals are vertebrates.</u>

b Nutrition:
_____

c Respiration:
_____

d Reproduction:
_____

e Physical characteristics:
_____

15

5 Use the information about fish and birds to complete the Venn diagram.

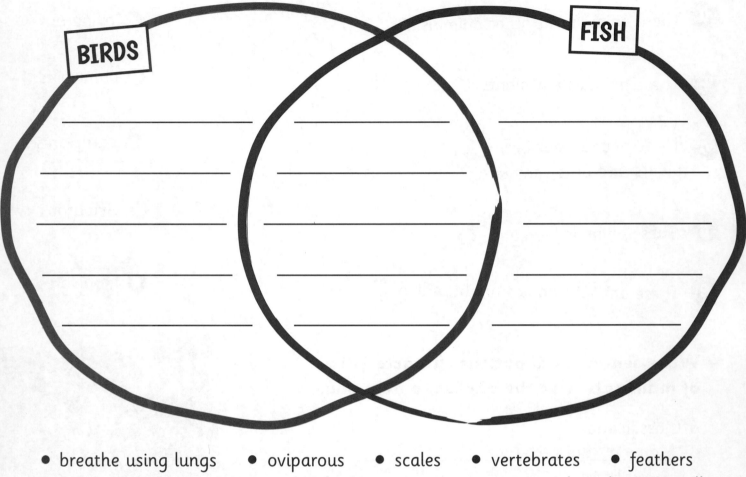

- breathe using lungs • oviparous • scales • vertebrates • feathers
- fins • wings • carnivores, herbivores or omnivores • breathe using gills

6 Read the text about amphibians and answer the questions.

Amphibians are oviparous and lay their eggs in water. Baby amphibians live in water and breathe through their gills. They change and grow into adults through a process called metamorphosis. Adult amphibians live both on land and in the water. Adults breathe with their lungs, but they also take in oxygen through their moist skin. Their gills close during metamorphosis.

a Where do baby amphibians live?

_____

b Where do adult amphibians live?

_____

c What is the name of the process by which baby amphibians change into adult amphibians?

_____

d How do adult amphibians breathe?

_____

7 Circle true (T) or false (F). Correct the false sentences.

a Turtles, snakes and crocodiles are reptiles.   T / F

_____

b Reptiles are viviparous.   T / F

_____

c Most reptiles are herbivores.   T / F

_____

d Reptiles breathe through their moist skin.   T / F

_____

e Reptiles lay their eggs in water.   T / F

_____

8 Read the clues and complete the crossword.

ACROSS

1 These animals use gills to breathe when they are young, but use their lungs and moist skin to breathe when they are adults.

2 These animals have fins, gills and scales.

DOWN

3 These animals are born live and drink their mother's milk.

4 Some of these animals do not have any legs.

5 These animals have feathers and most of them can fly.

9 Classify the invertebrates using the words in the box.

| cephalopod | crustacean | bivalve | arachnid | gastropod | insect |

a

insect

b

c

_____

d

e

f

_____

Which group of arthropods is missing? _____

10 Complete the sentences using the words in the box.

scorpions   shell
two   invertebrates
myriapods

a The majority of animals on Earth are _____ .

b Insects have _____ antennae.

c _____ have many pairs of legs.

d Some molluscs have a _____ for protection.

e Spiders and _____ are arachnids.

18

11 Circle the odd one out. Explain why it is different.

a pig / sheep / horse / (lizard)
Lizards are reptiles, whereas the others are mammals.

b bee / butterfly / spider / ant
_____

c frog / chameleon / toad / salamander
_____

d snail / tortoise / snake / crocodile
_____

e gastropod / bivlave / cephalopod / insect
_____

12 Unscramble the letters to find the words.

a All arthropods have this for protection. notsoxeleke _____

b Gastropods belong to this group. usomllcs _____

c Crustaceans have four of these body parts. natenean _____

d Invertebrates do not have this. kabeconb _____

13 Read the text. Choose a word from the box.
Write the correct word to the letters.

Salmon live in fresh water
and salt water. They are born
in freshwater habitats, such
as lakes or **(a)** _____ .
Salmon are oviparous and lay
(b) _____ . They are omnivores
and eat other fish, invertebrates
and plankton. **(c)** _____ are
predators of salmon.

bears

eggs

rivers

bees

4 HOW DO PLANTS GET THEIR FOOD?

1 Use the words in the box to label the plant.

stem   leaves   roots   flower

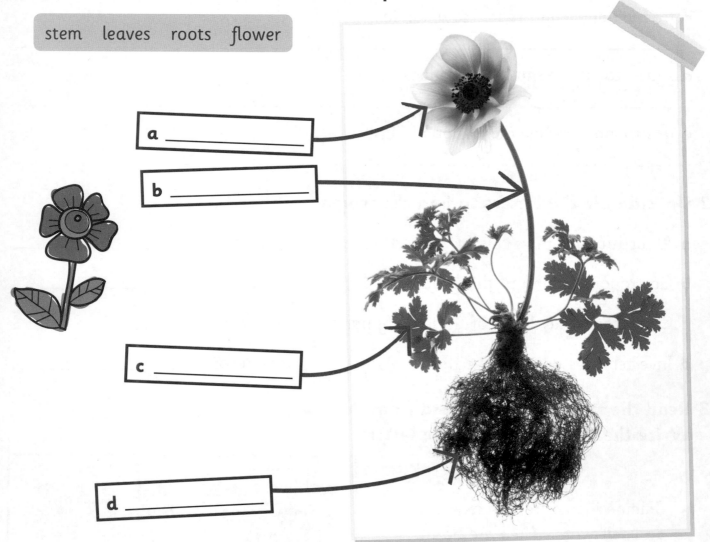

a _____

b _____

c _____

d _____

2 Read the definitions and write the words from Activity 1.

   a These are usually green. They help the plant make its food. _____

   b These absorb water and minerals from the soil. _____

   c This contains the plant's reproductive organs. _____

   d This gives the plant support. Water and nutrients are transported through this. _____

3 Classify the plants in the photos as a _tree_, _bush_ or _grass_.

a

b

c

grass

d

e

f

4 Match to make true sentences.

a Trees have high branches and a hard, ○   ○ short, thin stem.

b Bushes have low ○   ○ branches.

c Grasses usually have a ○   ○ than one hard stem.

d Many bushes have more ○   ○ thick stem called a trunk.

5 Classify the plants as *flowering* or *non-flowering*.

a _____ b _____ c _____ d _____

6 Decide if the sentences describe *angiosperms*, *gymnosperms* or *both*.

a They reproduce.   _____both_____

b Their seeds grow inside fruit.   _____

c They have roots, a stem and leaves.   _____

d The seeds grow inside cones.   _____

7 Read the text about mosses and answer the questions.

Mosses are very interesting plants. They do not have any flowers or seeds. They reproduce with tiny spores. They release the spores into the air and the wind carries them to places where they can begin to grow.

a Are mosses flowering or non-flowering plants?

_____

b What do they have that help them reproduce?

_____

c How does the wind help their reproduction?

_____

_____

_____

8 Find the words about plant classification in the wordsearch.

G	Y	M	N	O	S	P	E	R	M
R	R	S	T	U	U	W	F	A	Z
A	N	G	I	O	S	P	E	R	M
S	A	F	I	T	W	D	G	M	Q
S	E	E	D	S	T	N	S	O	R
E	T	R	Q	P	I	R	U	S	H
S	B	N	G	O	D	Q	E	S	U
Q	V	S	J	R	H	G	T	E	A
U	D	H	Q	E	R	Y	U	S	S
C	H	B	U	S	H	E	S	A	H

bushes
mosses
gymnosperm
seeds
ferns
angiosperm
grasses
trees
spores

9 Complete the sentences using the words in the box.

photosynthesis   stem   oxygen   ~~water and minerals~~
light energy   food   carbon dioxide   leaves

a The roots absorb __water and minerals__ from the soil.

b The water and minerals are transported up the _____ to the leaves.

c The plant takes in _____ and carbon dioxide through the _____ .

d The energy from the sun combines the water, minerals and _____ to make food. This process is called _____ .

e The _____ is then transported to all parts of the plant.

f When the plant makes its food, it also produces _____ .

10 Draw the arrows on the diagram to show the process of photosynthesis.

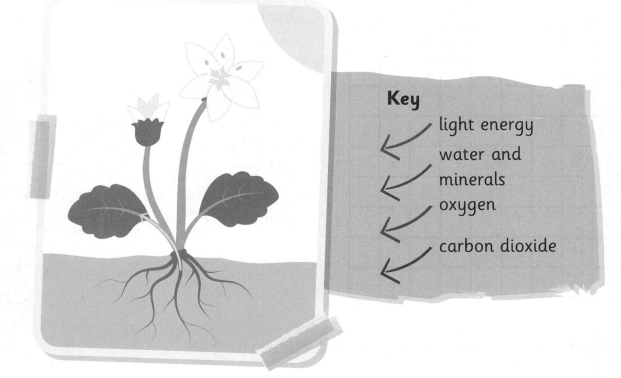

Key

light energy

water and minerals

oxygen

carbon dioxide

11 Label the diagram of a flower.

sepal carpel stigma stamen petal ovary

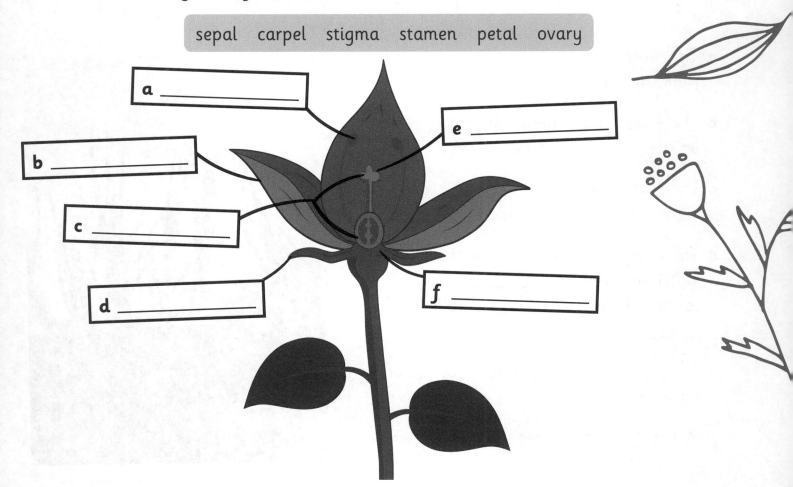

a _____

b _____

c _____

d _____

e _____

f _____

12 Circle true (T) or false (F). Correct the false sentences.

a All plants have flowers.   T / F

_____

b The petals protect the flower before it opens.   T / F

_____

c In flowering plants, the stamens produce pollen.   T / F

_____

d In flowering plants, the seeds grow inside the stem.   T / F

_____

13 Read the text. Choose the right words and write them on the lines.

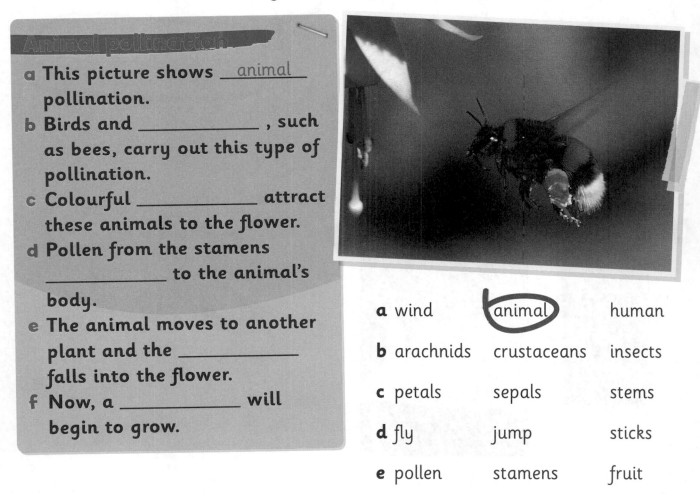

Animal pollination

a This picture shows ___animal___ pollination.

b Birds and _____ , such as bees, carry out this type of pollination.

c Colourful _____ attract these animals to the flower.

d Pollen from the stamens _____ to the animal's body.

e The animal moves to another plant and the _____ falls into the flower.

f Now, a _____ will begin to grow.

a wind   (animal)   human

b arachnids   crustaceans   insects

c petals   sepals   stems

d fly   jump   sticks

e pollen   stamens   fruit

f stem   root   seed

25

5 CAN YOU HELP SAVE THE PLANET?

1 Complete the study map using the words in the box.

insulator   state   ~~liquid~~   mixtures   gas

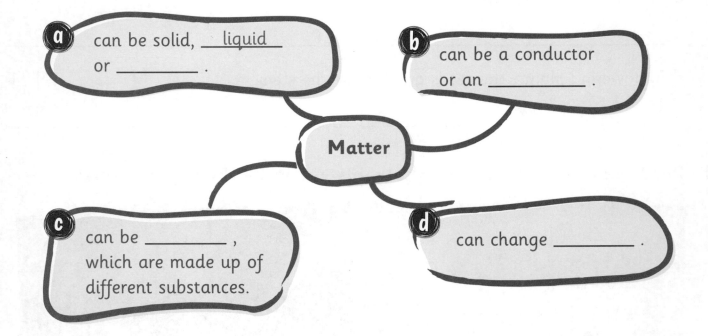

a can be solid, __liquid__ or _____ .

b can be a conductor or an _____ .

Matter

c can be _____ , which are made up of different substances.

d can change _____ .

2 Identify the states of matter inside these containers.

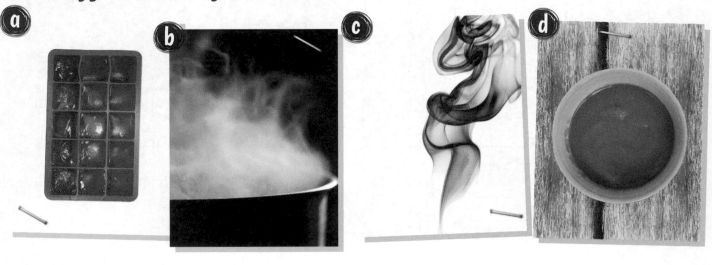

a   **b**   **c**   **d**

_____solid_____   _____   _____   _____

3 Match the definitions to the pictures.

1 Freezing: When we cool a liquid, it changes into a solid.

2 Evaporation: When we heat a liquid, it changes into a gas.

3 Melting: When we heat a solid, it changes into a liquid.

4 Complete the sentences using the words in the box.

liquid   ice   gas   definite   does not   ~~state~~   volume

a Matter can change _____state_____ .

b When we freeze water, it becomes _____ .

c When we heat a _____ , it changes into a _____ .

d A gas _____ have a definite shape or a definite _____ .

5 Complete the crossword.

ACROSS

1 When water changes into a gas, it becomes water _____ .

2 Everything is made up of _____ .

3 A _____ has a definite volume, but not a definite shape.

DOWN

4 Air is a _____ .

5 A _____ has a definite shape and a definite volume.

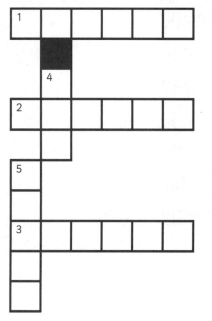

6 Match the forms of energy to the correct pictures.

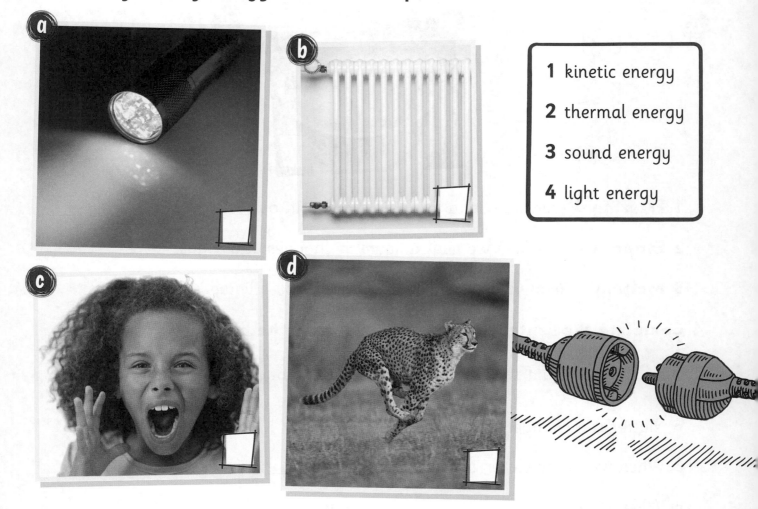

1 kinetic energy

2 thermal energy

3 sound energy

4 light energy

**7 Find the five forms of energy in the wordsearch.
Use the clues to help you.**

Q	K	T	G	S	M	D	F	E	Q
G	I	B	A	H	F	S	E	S	I
T	N	A	A	I	E	V	G	O	B
S	E	J	L	D	H	A	F	U	F
A	T	H	E	R	M	A	L	N	A
L	I	G	H	T	Q	V	B	D	X
O	C	P	O	U	S	A	G	Q	M
G	T	E	F	G	B	Z	A	D	W
N	P	G	B	S	A	E	T	H	M
E	L	E	C	T	R	I	C	A	L

a When we sing we produce this form of energy.

b A moving object contains this form of energy.

c The sun is a natural source of these forms of energy.

d A lot of machines need this form of energy to work.

8 Identify the forms of energy that these machines produce using electrical energy.

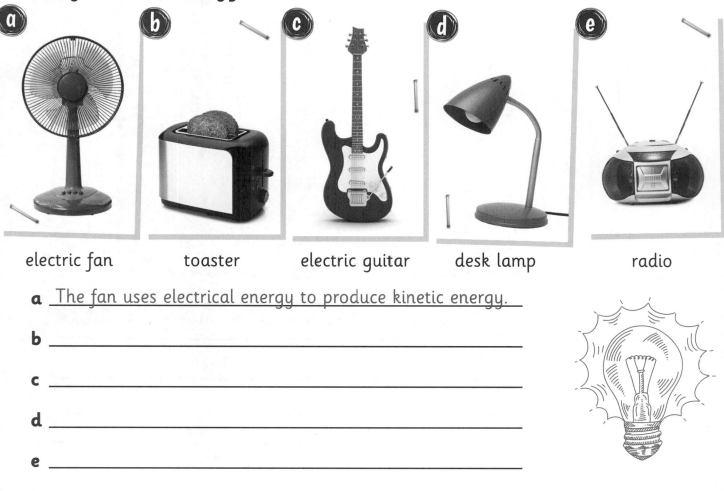

electric fan   toaster   electric guitar   desk lamp   radio

a _The fan uses electrical energy to produce kinetic energy._

b _____

c _____

d _____

e _____

9 Explain why we use wooden spoons for cooking.

We use wooden spoons for cooking because _____

_____

10 Which material is the odd one out? Circle the word and explain why.

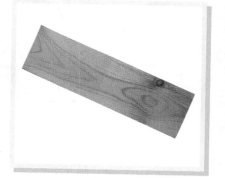

wool   wood   metal

_____

11 Read the menu and classify the mixtures.

MENU

~~Tomato soup~~

Vegetable stir-fry

Pasta salad

Paella

Strawberry milkshake

Fruit juice

Coffee

I can see the different substances.	I cannot see the different substances.
	Tomato soup

12 How can we separate these mixtures? Match.

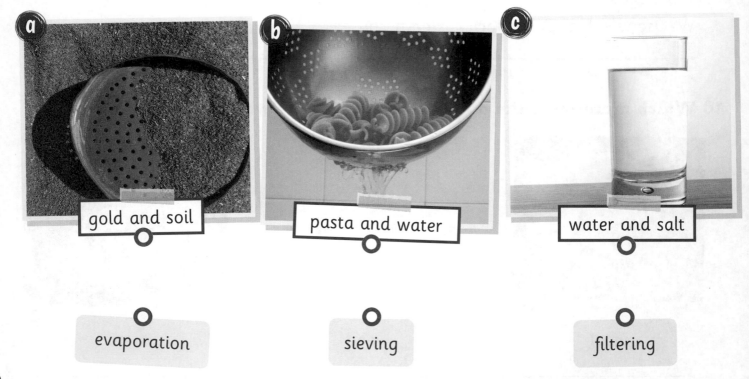

a) gold and soil

b) pasta and water

c) water and salt

evaporation

sieving

filtering

13 Read the text. Choose a word from the box. Write the correct word next to the letters a–d. There is one example.

planet   soil   supermarket   glass   walk   drive   wash   shower   soap   bike

My family knows that pollution is a serious problem for our ___planet___ .
These are some of the ways we help look after the environment:

- We always separate our waste into plastic, **(a)** _____ and paper, and put them in the right recycling bins.

- When we go shopping in the **(b)** _____ , we never ask for plastic bags. We take our own fabric bags from home.

- My school is near my house, so I can **(c)** _____ there with my brother. We have a car, but my mother and father go to work by bus.

- It is very important to save water. I always have a **(d)** _____ because baths use too much water.

Now choose the best name for the text. Tick one box.

Taking care of the planet ☐

Going to the supermarket ☐

Helping at home ☐

WHAT IS A *SIMPLE MACHINE*?

1 Match to make true sentences.

a Machines ○

○ are made up of simple machines.

b Complex machines ○

○ have no moving parts or few moving parts.

c Simple machines ○

○ make work easier.

2 Identify the simple machines in the photos.

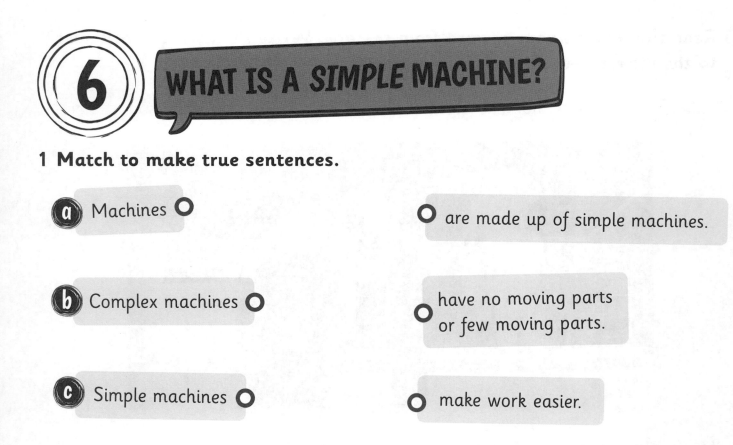

a

b

c

This is a pulley. _____

d

e

f

_____ _____ _____

3 Complete each sentence with the correct simple machine.

a A _____screw_____ hold things together and also lifts objects.

b A _____ is made up of a rigid bar and a support called a fulcrum.

c A _____ has a slanted surface. We use it to cut things.

d A _____ is made up of a rope and a wheel.

e An _____ is a surface that goes from a low level to a high level.

f A _____ is a wheel which turns around an axle.

4 Match each diagram to the correct real-life example.

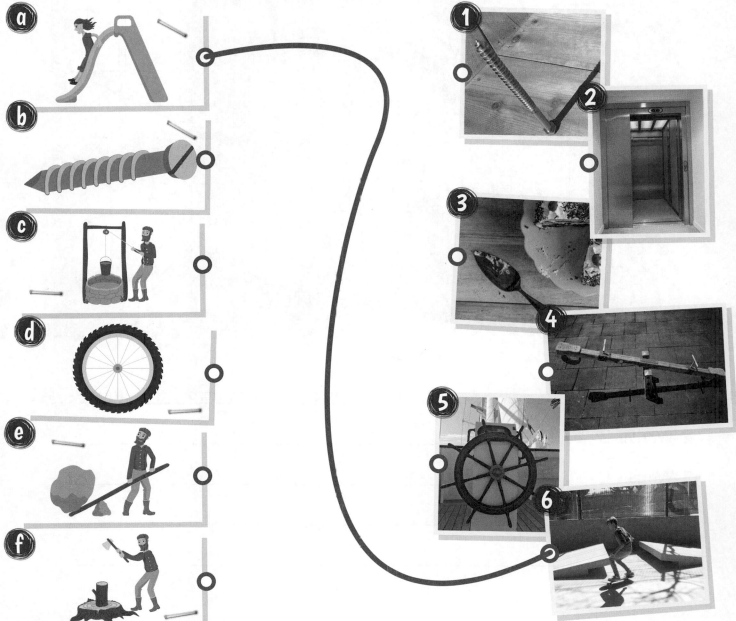

5 Can you help these people? Which simple machine should they use?

1 Worker A needs ___wheels and axles to move the boxes across the ground.___

2 Worker B needs _____

3 Worker C _____

4 Worker D _____

5 Worker E _____

6 Become a machine detective! Investigate simple machines at school.

There are simple machines all around us at school. Do not forget that complex machines are made up of simple machines.

How many simple machines can you find? Complete the chart below.

Drawing	Simple machines
	This is the slide in the playground. It is an inclined plane.

7 What do we use these complex machines for? Draw more examples.

transport　communication　entertainment　housework

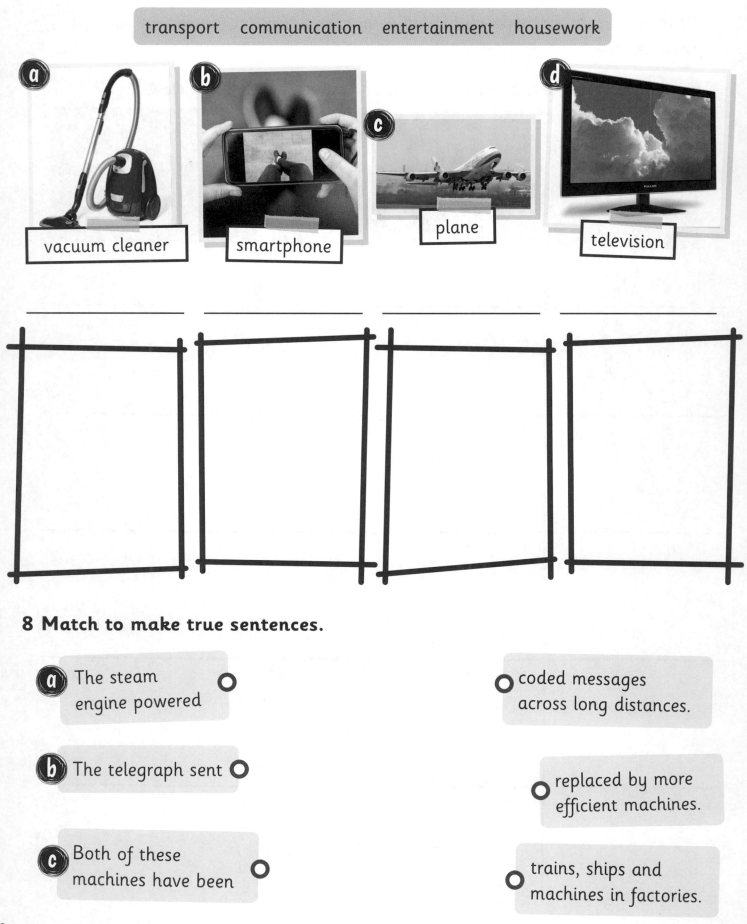

a　vacuum cleaner

b　smartphone

c　plane

d　television

8 Match to make true sentences.

a The steam engine powered ○　　○ coded messages across long distances.

b The telegraph sent ○　　○ replaced by more efficient machines.

c Both of these machines have been ○　　○ trains, ships and machines in factories.

9 Choose the correct words and write them on the lines.

a This is a lever that children sit on to move up and down. You find it in a playground. ___seesaw___

b This machine is made up of a lever and a wedge. We use it for digging. _____

c This contains a wheel and axle. You find it in a playground. _____

d This is an inclined plane that children use in a playground. _____

e This converts electrical energy into light energy. It has a screw that we use to attach it to a lamp. _____

f This complex machine contains wheels and axles. We use it for transport. _____

light bulb

slide

seesaw

spade

bicycle

roundabout

10 Look at the picture and read the story. Write words to complete the sentences about the story. You can use 1, 2, 3 or 4 words.

My name is Dan and I go to school with my friends Pam and Esther. One day, we were on our way home from school when we saw my brother Paul in the playground. He was on the seesaw with his friend. They were moving up and down.

We all went on the roundabout together. We went so fast that when we got off and got on our bikes, we all fell over because we were so dizzy.

a In the playground, Dan and his friends went on the _____ .

b Dan's friends are called _____ .

c When Dan arrived at the playground his _____ on the seesaw.

d They all fell off their bikes because they _____ .

Try writing these words in your own language!

Unit 1
Why do babies have more bones than adults?

bone (n) _____

brain (n) _____

contract (v) _____

control (v) _____

hearing (n) _____

inner ear (n) _____

interact (v) _____

joint (n) _____

middle ear (n) _____

muscle (n) _____

nerve (n) _____

nervous system (n) _____

nostril (n) _____

olfactory nerve (n) _____

outer ear (n) _____

pupil (n) _____

retina (n) _____

relax (v) _____

sensory nerve (n) _____

sight (n) _____

signal (n) _____

skeleton (n) _____

skin (n) _____

smell (n) _____

taste (n) _____

touch (n) _____

taste bud (n) _____

Unit 2
What happens to food inside your body?

artery (n) _____

atrium (n) _____

bladder (n) _____

carbon dioxide (n) _____

circulatory system (n) _____

concentrate (v) _____

develop (v) _____

digestive system (n) _____

excretory system (n) _____

exercise (n) _____

intestine (n) _____

healthy habits (n) _____

kidney (n) _____

lung (n) _____

mood (n) _____

nutrient (n) _____

organ (n) _____

oxygen (n) _____

respiratory system (n) _____

self-esteem (n) _____

stomach (n) _____

urethra (n) _____

urine (n) _____

vein (n) _____

ventricle (n) _____

waste (n) _____

Unit 3
Which vertebrate has *two lives*?

amphibian (n) _____

arachnid (n) _____

arthropod (n) _____

backbone (n) _____

bird (n) _____

bivalve (n) _____

carnivore (n) _____

cephalopod (n) _____

crustacean (n) _____

exoskeleton (n) _____

fin (n) _____

fish (n) _____

gastropod (n) _____

gill (n) _____

herbivore (n) _____

invertebrate (n) _____

mammal (n) _____

metamorphosis (n) _____

mollusc (n) _____

myriapod (n) _____

omnivore (n) _____

oviparous (adj) _____

reptile (n) _____

scale (n) _____

shell (n) _____

vertebrate (n) _____

viviparous (adj) _____

Unit 4
How do plants get their food?

angiosperm (n) _____

bush (n) _____

carpel (n) _____

cone (n) _____

deciduous (adj) _____

evergreen (adj) _____

fern (n) _____

flower (n) _____

flowering plant (n) _____

fruit (n) _____

grass (n) _____

gymnosperm (n) _____

leaf (n) _____

moss (n) _____

non-flowering plant (n) _____

ovary (n) _____

petal (n) _____

photosynthesis (n) _____

pollen (n) _____

pollination (n) _____

root (n) _____

seed (n) _____

sepal (n) _____

spore (n) _____

stamen (n) _____

stem (n) _____

stigma (n) _____

tree (n) _____

Unit 5
Can you help save the planet?

conductor (n) _____

cool (v) _____

dissolve (v) _____

electrical energy (n) _____

energy (n) _____

evaporate (v) _____

filter (v) _____

freeze (v) _____

gas (n) _____

heat (v) _____

ice (n) _____

insulator (n) _____

kinetic energy (n) _____

light energy (n) _____

liquid (n) _____

matter (n) _____

mixture (n) _____

property (n) _____

separate (v) _____

shape (n) _____

sieve (v) _____

solid (n) _____

sound energy (n) _____

thermal energy (n) _____

volume (n) _____

water (n) _____

water vapour (n) _____

Unit 6
What is a *simple* machine?

bar (n) _____

code (n) _____

complex (adj) _____

fulcrum (n) _____

handle (n) _____

heavy (adj) _____

hold (v) _____

inclined plane (n) _____

invention (n) _____

lever (n) _____

lift (v) _____

lower (v) _____

machine (n) _____

message (n) _____

Morse code (n) _____

pulley (n) _____

rigid (adj) _____

rope (n) _____

screw (n) _____

simple machine (n) _____

slanted (adj) _____

steam engine (n) _____

surface (n) _____

telegraph (n) _____

tie (v) _____

wedge (n) _____

wheel and axle (n) _____